Legal

ISBN: 978-1-7321877-7-1

This publication is designed to provide accurate and authoritative information in regard to the subject matter covered. It is sold with the understanding that neither the author nor the publisher is engaged in rendering legal, accounting, or other professional service. If legal advice or other expert assistance is required, the services of a competent professional person should be sought.

Table of Contents

Introduction

I recently found several early letters that I sent to Warren Buffett and other people that I was interested in connecting with based on their business and/or corporate philosophy.

Fire Dragon

The fire dragon has been awakened from its slumber again.
Thank you LT.

Warren Buffett

Without further adieu: Communication to Warren Buffett.

Matthew L. Myers
P.O. Box 300354
Kaaawa, HI 96730

April 9, 2008

Warren E. Buffett
1440 Kiewit Plaza
Omaha, Nebraska 68131

Re: In The Unlikely Event That This Letter Finds Its Way To Your Desk

Dear Mr. Buffet:

I have been following your career as an investor for a couple of years, and greatly admire your integrity. Your criticisms of the overvaluation of top managers and your willingness to purchase stocks/other assets for the long-term continue to hold up despite a consensus viewpoint, which often differs.

A New York Times article indicated that you are "seeking a new (and younger) candidate for a top investing position." I have thought about your proposition for over a year. What would I write or say that could possibly capture your attention?

I am very adept at observation regarding traffic/material goods flow both for their potential and limitations.

As an example: I have observed a rural railroad facility that distributes coal, cattle and wall-board, determining that an area or region has untapped resources (wood from overgrown deserted farmland that could easily be harvested and sold for pulp wood at a minimal cost; concluding that a company (railroad) or region may not be maximizing its potential for profit from unused resources (unfilled railroad cars that could be filed with pulp wood extracted from undervalued deserted farmland).

I have always had the ability to see what the value of a company actually is, not what the perception might be.

My undergraduate work was done at Cornell University. I am completing an Executive MBA at the University of Hawaii with an emphasis on the Pacific Rim. My experiences here in both the workplace and living environment have made me very sensitive to the nuances of Asian culture encompassing continental Asia and Asian-America.

My proposal is as follows: I am interested in setting up a Berkshire Hathaway Office to monitor investment opportunities that are not country specific. The office would be located here in the Pacific to analyze distribution and logistics issues. It would be close enough to assess a company's asset potential in a tangible and physical manner (i.e. flying to an undervalued company in any Asian country to review its capabilities).

The office would conduct site visits of undervalued companies and assess them in comparison to their annual reports. The review of a corporation's stock price, annual report and other paper instruments (income statements, balance sheets or financial performance ratios) of the company would be conducted after visiting their manufacturing facilities to order to obtain an unbiased first impression.

I think that I can increase the asset base of Berkshire Hathaway and I think that I can do it far more cost effectively than other fund managers. I am not getting an opportunity to do this now and would like to do so.

Thank you.

Aloha,

Matthew

I was interested in working for Warren (WB) early in my career. His folksy hard-nosed approach was always attractive from a business management perspective. His investment strategy is ruthless and unforgiving. It requires no explanation.

As such, the title of the letter and this book *In The Unlikely Event That This Finds Its Way To Your Desk*. At this time I was in the Pacific.

Naturally I didn't hear anything back and it is in fact unlikely that he read the letter. However, it served as a formulation of a personal business, economic and policy strategy formation.

The question remains: Did WB actually receive the letter or not?

Only portions of the letter are quoted directly due to the professional military references and military work.

Included are the releasable quotes from my correspondence.

"My experience covers a varied range of Public Policy issues ranging from budget and finance, procurement, agriculture, urban and land use planning, water and waste water, low- and moderate-income housing, renewable energy, environmental design, transportation and national defense.

Public policy issues that I have worked on entailed projects for the City and County of Honolulu, Department of Budget and Fiscal Services, the State of Hawaii Departments of Business, Economic Development and Tourism, Land and Natural Resources, Health and the Office of Hawaiian affairs; and on military issues for the relocation of the Marine Corps.

On the national level I have also worked on public policy issues in Washington for Congressman Amory Houghton; and Congressman Maurice Hinchey in Upstate New York.

I recently completed my Executive MBA (evenings and weekends) at the University of Hawai'i at Manoa, Shidler College of Business. My undergraduate degree in Applied Economics and Business Management was obtained from Cornell University with Honors. I was a 2008 Washofsky Scholarship recipient from the Shidler College of Business University of Hawaii at Manoa. While at UH I completed a comprehensive financial and organizational (structure and internal processes) analysis of Bank of Hawaii and First

Hawaiian Bank; a feasibility and implementation analysis for a large scale photovoltaic (PV) installation for a regional (10% of overall market) dental group (Hawaii Family Dental Centers); and an analysis of venture capital trends.

My major strength is that I am receptive to things that are quantified but that are not perceived by existing managers. Two recent examples are: (1) for the Bank of Hawaii I discovered specific joint-venture initiatives that the company could use to address future growth; and (2) for the solar industry my research uncovered a 2.5% tariff that the industry hadn't addressed (and wasn't even paying) as a part of its cost valuations, which could prevent future market entrants from incurring "hidden" costs that would impair or hinder their profitability over the long-term.

The dynamics of an organization are critical to its effective operation. A cabinet member should be complimented by the operational systems that support, surround and enhance employers engaged in this work. As a cabinet member I can bring a unique, stand-alone and distinctive perspective on further streamlining operations, while integrating other processes and perspectives to form new and unique team-solidifying synergies that enhance the financial performance of the company.

I have comprehensive experience with the City and County of Honolulu, Department of Budget and Fiscal Services and the State of Hawaii in the areas of procurement, financial and budgetary management, land use development and planning. In each area of employment I completely reorganized operations, reduced fiscal and budgetary waste and removed programmatic redundancies."

The result of this letter was an interview, which went well, but didn't result in me being hired. However, one of the questions was as follows: "Why is someone like yourself from NY and with your experience working at the City and County of Honolulu?" The major politician (elected to office) spotted me later when I was walking toward him and jumped in the bushes to hide and avoid me. Imagine that! How cool. Some people are naturally threatened and competitive. It is human nature.

I have submitted lots of other similar carefully crafted letters to many other corporations, each has been instrumental in shaping my thinking and philosophical approach; or insights that I uncovered or experiences as a part of a team.

Many of them resulted in interviews. Most did not. In life, as a philosophy, it is important to never give up. The letter above was far too long. Get to the point. This is how I look back on the correspondence now.

I have always been interested in government, policy and economic development. My experience working with different agencies in government has reflected this.

Letter to President Barack Obama

I wrote to Barack Obama's administration in 2013.

President Barack Obama
The White House
1600 Pennsylvania Avenue NW
Washington, DC 20500

December 1, 2013

Matthew L. Myers
CEO/Founder
Infrastructure Upgrade, Inc.

Dear President Obama,

Infrastructure Upgrade, Inc. has developed a disruptive mobile application that links the public and private sectors allowing consumers, businesses and government to recommend and develop innovative infrastructure improvements that they would like to see in their neighborhoods and communities. Categories include airports, railroads, roads, bridges, schools and housing.

The app is live at: https://itunes.apple.com/us/app/upgrade-it!/id672622614.

Our site is located at: http://www.infrastructureupgrade.com.

Our enterprise app is forthcoming.

We look forward to hearing from you.

Thank you.

Sincerely,

Matthew L. Myers
CEO and Founder
Infrastructure Upgrade, Inc.

Bi-Partisan Support for President Obama

Infrastructure is a mission critical initiative. The letter speaks for itself.

Letter to President Trump

I wrote to Donald Trump's administration in 2016.

Twitter & Associated Attachment

Donald Trump and Team,

Congratulations on the Presidency

Our team has tools and a plan for $2 trillion U.S. #infrastructure #backlog - including #FlintWaterCrisis

Our team can be reached at http://www.infrastructureupgrade.com and/or http://www.iuienterprise.com

Thank you.

Best regards,

Matthew
CEO and Founder
Infrastructure Upgrade, Inc.

Current Administration Infrastructure Support

Infrastructure is essential to the U.S and world economies. The letter speaks for itself. The format was Twitter®. The medium was selected intentionally based on its target audience, one that requires *very* simple communication.

Family History With Promoting Democracy and Tackling Difficult Issues

In other instances professional colleagues or friends have asked me to submit written testimony on their behalf. These have included a U.S. Commanding General, a Public Utilities Commissioner; or specific bills relating to energy conservation, and/or ocean debris.

A friend in the San Francisco Bay area asked me to weigh in maintaining and preserving Democracy in Hong Kong. As this is something of paramount importance and a hallmark of my upbringing it was easy to do for her.

My family, like President George Bush and his heirs, are founders of the United States. He liked to state that he had two hereditary lines to the Mayflower. In my lineage there are three lines that were instrumental in designing, planning and building the country's bridges and physical infrastructure. These are the very same structures that connect every aspect of the United States from Coast to Coast, generating commerce and economic activity that has made this a truly distinct and strong nation.

The promotion of Democracy, civic equality and diplomacy are family traditions dating back more than 400+ years, earlier than the signing of the Declaration of Independence and the Constitution.

The author standing in front of the Liberty Bell, Philadelphia, Pennsylvania.

My grandmother (and grandfather) passed this guidance on to me (which had been provided to them). I in turn will continue this tradition for the next generation, including my own children.

My grandmother wrote several books, including one on the Underground Railroad and hosted the son of an African chief in their home in the 1960s in rural upstate New York. This was considered very daring and controversial at the time.

I intend to continue this tradition. It seems more important than ever in this political and economic environment. The attacks against groups of very different and diverse groups of people *have worsened*, not improved.

History repeats itself.

The fascism of Germany, Italy and Russia in World War II and the ethnic genocides of Rwanda, Cambodia and Yugoslavia (Bosnia) have no place in a varied and thriving world. These are just examples of human conduct gone horribly awry. Sadly there are too many examples to cite here, including South Africa and now India and China.

At home in the United States the violent attacks on African Americans during the Civil Rights movement have become more mechanized recently, and expanded to include Jews, Muslims and other religious groups. This is *unequivocally unacceptable*.

Reversing Intolerance

This trend can and must be reversed, in part, through aggressive education (learning about unique customs and traditions through reading, language, music, cuisine, sport and how to conduct oneself – removing shoes before entering a home in Japan) and an economy that is inclusive for all (livable wage, et. al.).

Creating Diversions: Misguided Public Policy

Rural populations, which typically may also include minorities, and/or low- and moderate-income communities, are also the target of discrimination and abusive behavior by the government industrial complex.

Nuclear Spent Fuel Site Selection

When I was in high school, my rural upstate New York community was selected to store low-level radioactive waste (a semantics misnomer explained later in the text) and ultimately the high-level spent reactor fuel. Most of which is repurposed worldwide for weapons programs.

$4,000 for Hospital and Funeral Expenses: Per Person

After further due diligence, discovery and lawsuits the following was revealed in the government planning documentation and risk assessment: Each member of my rural farm community) was worth approximately $4,000.00 for a stochastic radiation fatality.

This is the United Government's documented willingness to pay (WTP) for human loss of life (a chart provided as a part of the legal discovery process) associated from radiation deaths from spent reactor fuel. The government intended to place the facility on a farm (in an open field) over a major earthquake fault line and massive water aquifer.

Comparative Cost Analysis

When I worked in Washington, D.C. years later this $4,000.00 didn't even cover the cost of a *single luncheon* for the lobbyists and public officials shaping policy that would never impact them or their families.

Recent Financial Comparison

As a more recent comparison, this cost covered a three (3) three hour visit for my father to go to the nearby hospital. A family of four is only worth $20K (approximately $4,000 each to the United States government).

Essentially for those individuals selected to house a spent reactor facility and/or impacted by a rail spill transporting the material across the country *are materially worthless.*

Farms, ranches, cattle, crops and other business are also *without any value*. Many of the farms, in the rural upstate New York community selected for the repository, were owned and operated by their families for over 200 years.

The current Permian Basin site selection proposal in New Mexico and Texas will place communities along major industrial rail lines throughout the country at high risk from train derailments.[1]

It also has the potential to irradiate the shale oil reserves in the area, undermining national security and the country's ability to reduce its dependence on foreign fossil fuels. Powering U.S. vehicles with *radioactive gasoline* is not a good strategy

100,000-Year Storage Problem

The length of high-level spent reactor fuel's radioactive life is 100,000 years, requiring safe storage far beyond recorded human history, including the Torah, Bible, Koran and other major written texts.

---

[1]Nuclear waste fight brewing in the Permian Basin. *OK Energy Today*. August 15, 2019. http://www.okenergytoday.com/2019/08/nuclear-waste-fight-brewing-in-the-permian-basin/.

The pyramids are one of the only known structures known to have lasted more than 5,000 years.

Financial Ruin and Disaster

Over and over again humanity has seen the results of problems with nuclear technology and its failed storage: bankruptcies ($9 billion in losses for Westinghouse/Toshiba), cost overruns ($98 billion spent on Yucca Mountain, Nevada and $9 billion in South Carolina) and entire communities forced to vacate their irradiated homes and businesses.

These include, but are not limited to, Chernobyl, Pryp'yat', Three Mile Island Nuclear Generating Station in Dauphin County, Pennsylvania, Fukishima Daiichi, Japan, Tokai, Ibaraki Prefecture, Japan, Mayak, Ozersk, Russia, Goiânia, and the State of Goiás, Brazil.

With rising sea levels the world can expect more total meltdowns and complete loss of life. Most reactors are located in coastal regions.

Spent Reactor Fuel's Pipeline for Weapons Programs

Spent reactor fuel is not waste.

It serves one purpose: to be reprocessed to build weapons to annihilate entire cities and countries.

Expertise

I grew up listening to the work of the designer and architect of the world's *smallest and largest nuclear weapons.* **High-level spent reactor fuel requires walls of solid lead that are nine (9) feet thick** on each side and including the roof enclosure. This is 27 feet of lead multiplied by a structure required to store 210,000 tons of waste.[2]

Subsurface water tables are the perfect transport mechanism for radioactive isotopes (i.e. radionuclides) as water travels through rock and earth.

Radioactive water is easily ingested and immediately begins damaging internal organs of animals, particularly humans.

---

[2]Nuclear waste fight brewing in the Permian Basin. OK Energy Today. August 15, 2019. http://www.okenergytoday.com/2019/08/nuclear-waste-fight-brewing-in-the-permian-basin/.

This requires a massive lead mine and structure larger than several football stadiums. One of the most stable architectural structures in human history is the pyramid in Egypt.

Showcasing the exceptional architectural design of the Egyptians. The Metropolitan Museum of Art, New York, NY.

Spent reactor fuel is the ultimate tar baby: A technology that is beyond control.

What Did This Result In? Stepping Forward

Based on my upbringing, family's early guidance and on-going legal work (and more recently LT's Hong Kong request): These written responses were cathartic and have resulted in a flood of communication activity.

The *one life* does matter.

It is essential to stand strong, even in the face of Goliath, *using the pen not the sword*. Violence *does not* solve public policy, United States and international law does.

Democracy in Hong Kong

A letter to the following: various U.S. Senate and House members regarding Hong Kong, including the U.S. Senate Intelligence Committee.

Matthew Myers
P.O. Box 289
Lakeville, CT 06039

August 3, 2019

Re: In support of S. 1838: Hong Kong Human Rights and Democracy Act of 2019

Dear Messrs Jones, Kaine, Kennedy, Lankford, Leahy, Lee, Manchin, Markey, McConnell, Menedez, Merkley, Peters, Portman, Reed, Roberts, Moran, Rand, Perdue and Roberts, Jr.; and Mesdames McSally, Murkowski and Murray:

I am writing in support of the bi-partisan passage of S. 1838 Hong Kong Human Rights and Democracy Act of 2019. The promotion of democracy and democratic rule of law is a hallmark of U.S. foreign policy. I strongly support this proposed bill in maintaining and strengthening this tradition, not only in Hong Kong, but also throughout the world.

Thank you.

Sincerely,

Matthew L. Myers

Rationale and Thinking

The thought process behind the letter writing: Democratic rule of law is essential to a thriving economy. In the United States and abroad it has resulted in business innovation and exceptional economic growth. The list of Senators and Congressman and Congresswoman that received this written testimony is more extensive than this single example (all of them received letters).

However, to date not a single elected representative or their office has responded directly. Senator Mitch McConnell indirectly responded and wrote an Opinion piece on Hong Kong for *The Wall Street Journal.*

The one response that has been received is a generic email communication to provide general assistance on tours of the Capital and Washington and assistance on Congressional (HR) bills. This document is provided at the end of the letters.

Infrastructure in the United States

A letter to the following: various U.S. Senate and House members regarding Infrastructure policy in this country, including the U.S. Senate Intelligence Committee.

Matthew Myers
P.O. Box 289
Lakeville, CT 06039

August 1, 2019

Re: In support of H.R. 1428: Transportation Infrastructure for Job Creation Act

Dear Messrs Daines, Durbin, Enzi, Gardner, Graham, Grassley, Hawley, Hoeven, Isakson and Johnson; and Mesdames Ernest, Fisher, Gillibrand, Hassan, Hirono and Hyde-Smith,

I am writing in support of the bi-partisan passage of *H.R. 1428: Transportation Infrastructure for Job Creation Act*. The strengthening of America's infrastructure is a mission critical initiative providing tangible job-creation results, from the country's inception to the present.

Public works development was continued as a part of the extraordinary initiatives of President Franklin D. Roosevelt's New Deal and expanded with exceptional results under the guidance of President Dwight D. Eisenhower.

I strongly support this proposed bill in maintaining and strengthening this tradition, not only in this bill, but in future proposed legislation designed to fund and execute the next generation of state of the art railroads, bridges, ports, highways, dams and new military facilities.

My company Infrastructure Upgrade, Inc. located at http://www.infrastructureupgrade.com provides a platform to start the discussion and execute the results.

Thank you for your consideration.

Sincerely,

Matthew L. Myers

36

Rationale and Thinking

The conceptual framework behind the letter writing: Infrastructure is the core foundation to a thriving business economy. Poorly designed and executed infrastructure results in an economy that is dysfunctional and impaired.

Oceans in the United States

A letter to the following: various U.S. Senate and House members regarding Oceans policy in this country.

Matthew Myers
P.O. Box 289
Lakeville, CT 06039

August 3, 2019

Re: In support of S. 1982: Save Our Seas 2.0 Act

Dear Messrs Aderholt, Byrne, Brooks, Biggs, Bera, M.D., Crawford, Cook (Ret.), De Saulnier, Grijalva, Gosar, D.D.S., Gallego, Garamendi, Hill, Huffman, Harder, Lamelfa, McClintock, McNerney, O'Halleran, Palmer, Rogers, Schweikert, Stanton, Thompson, Womack, Westerman and Young and Mesdames Bass, Kirkpatrick, Lasko, Lee, Matsui, Pelosi, Ruby, Amata and Sewell,

I am writing in support of the bi-partisan passage of S. 1982: Save Our Seas 2.0 Act. The volume of plastic and marine debris has reached epidemic levels in the oceans, lakes and rivers of the United States, and throughout the world. On some beaches, there is no sand or rock visible due to the extraordinary amount of trash.

This impacts other areas of the economic vitality of communities: compromising fishing fleets and the quality of fish being processed (they are filled with plastic); and creates hazardous conditions in our ports, harbors, irrigation systems and dams.

Thank you.

Sincerely,

Matthew L. Myers

Rationale and Thinking

The business strategy behind the letter writing: Ocean based commerce is vital to the strength of the U.S. economy. The following all depend harbors and oceans: Fishing fleets and their catches, military operations, oil and container ships, and tourism and recreation. Anything that impairs their progress undermines the contributions that these activities make to Gross Domestic Product (GDP).

The letter was sent to other Senators and representatives.

Human Trafficking

A letter to the following: various U.S. Senate and House members regarding human trafficking policy in this country.

Matthew Myers
P.O. Box 289
Lakeville, CT 06039

July 30, 2019

Re: In support of H.R. 295: To increase the role of the financial industry in combating human trafficking

Dear Messrs Murphy, Blumenthal, Burr, Warner, Risch, Rubio, Wyden, Heinrich, Blunt, King, Cotton, Cornyn, Bennet, Sasse and Fitzpatrick; and Mesdames Waters, Gabbard, Ocasio-Cortez, Omar, Feinstein, Collins and Harris,

I am writing in support of the bi-partisan passage of H.R. 295: To increase the role of the financial industry in combating human trafficking. Involuntary captivity undermines community and regional stability, targeting women, children, minorities and other vulnerable populations in economically distressed regions and war-torn countries in the United States and throughout the world.

Legislation that takes the robust anti-money laundering (AML) compliance tools that the financial industry has at its disposal and enhances these controls is extremely valuable.

In extreme situations, enslaved women and children are used as weapons (Boko Haram) endangering U.S and NATO allied forces and United Nations peacekeeping missions and costing billions of dollars in intelligence, law enforcement and military deployments, while including the loss of human life.

These extremist groups efforts are severely impaired and undermined by stringent AML and banking controls (logins from multiple IP addresses) that limit their access to funds for weapons, supplies and transportation.

I strongly support this proposed bill in maintaining and strengthening this tradition, not only in this bill, but in future proposed legislation designed to execute the next generation of AML and banking controls.

Thank you for your consideration.

Sincerely,

Matthew L. Myers

Rationale and Thinking

The economic cost behind human trafficking to the United States and the world is staggering. Any legislation that strengthens the banking controls to cut off financing for the organizers of this activity is valuable.

Impeachment

A letter to the following: various U.S. Senate and House members regarding the Mueller Report and the impeachment of the President of the United States.

Matthew Myers
P.O. Box 289
Lakeville, CT 06039

August 1, 2019

H.Res. 13: Impeaching Donald John Trump, President of the United States,
for high crimes and misdemeanors.

Dear Messrs Cruz, Alexander, Barrasso, Booker, Boozman, Braun, Brown, Kramer, Cantwell, Cardin, Carper, Casey, Jr., Cassidy and Coons; and Mesdames Baldwin, Blackburn and Cortez Masto,

I am writing in support of the bi-partisan passage of H.Res. 13: Impeaching Donald John Trump, President of the United States, for high crimes and misdemeanors.

The Robert Mueller report (along with his outstanding team) provides a clear case for the impeachment of the current President of the United States for conduct unbefitting of an elected official.

I strongly support this proposed bill in maintaining and strengthening the rule of democratic law, upholding the Constitution and ensuring that foreign powers do not undermine the exceptional democratic process of the United States; not only in this bill, but in future proposed legislation designed to ensure that the Office of the President of the United States and his Administration are upheld to the highest standards of ethical and legal conduct.

Thank you for your consideration.

Sincerely,

Matthew L. Myers

Rationale and Thinking

An examination of the Mueller Report makes it clear: Robert Mueller and his team in cooperation with State and Federal government agencies and law enforcement completed an extraordinary report, making a clear case for impeachment of the current President of the United States. I recommend reading the document in its entirety if you haven't already done so.

Outcomes

The outcome of this process: One direct written responses and one indirect email newsletter for over four hundred hand signed and addressed letters.

One Congresswoman from my district provided the following email letter:

"August 30, 2019

Dear Matthew,

Thank you for contacting me with your thoughts on the impeachment of the President. I appreciate that you took the time to express your thoughts on this matter.

Like you, I deeply respect the Office of the President, and cherish the electoral process that allows an American to assume the Oval Office. I know that the integrity of the presidency, guarded by respect for our foundational laws and values, is more important than any one person or political party. I will always protect the sanctity of our democracy over the consideration of political or electoral implications.

Over the past two years, Special Counsel Mueller's investigation has led to charges filed against 37 individuals, and secured seven guilty pleas and one conviction at trial. Among these were six former associates and advisers of the President; their charges included financial crimes, working with foreign governments, and making false statements to the FBI and Congress.

After reviewing the Special Counsel's report, two things are abundantly clear: the Russian government launched an extended and intentional misinformation campaign to influence the 2016 American presidential election, and the President and members of his campaign apparatus committed egregious acts that undermined our judiciary system, put our national security at risk, and jeopardized the American people's trust in our electoral system.

The report also showed clear evidence that the President made efforts to obstruct the Special Counsel's investigation into this possible collusion. However, citing a longstanding Department of Justice policy that it is unconstitutional to charge a president with a federal crime while they are in office, the Special Counsel did not formally conclude whether or not the President obstructed justice.

As a career history teacher, I know the Constitution, and I know that no one is above the law. The Constitution provides checks and balances to Congress, the Executive branch, and the Judiciary to ensure that no branch of government can violate American laws and foundations without being held accountable. In the most serious cases, the Constitution entrusts Congress with the power to file articles of impeachment and remove a President from office – and these are serious times.

The President's behavior is not becoming of the Oval Office, and he has even said that he would take information from a foreign country if given the opportunity again. I believe that the actions detailed in the Special Counsel's report, along with this behavior, demand the utmost concern and immediate action from Congress. That is why I support a thorough investigation of the President's behavior, whether through the current investigations that my colleagues are leading or through an impeachment inquiry. This will allow Congress to gather all of the necessary information needed.

President Trump's openness to foreign interference is deeply concerning. Congress has a responsibility to investigate what

—

happened in the 2016 election and the administration's actions since that time. Those investigations must continue, and I would support an impeachment inquiry if that is where the facts take us. But first, Congress and the American people need to get all the information required.

Over the past few months, I have voted with my colleagues to pass House Concurrent Resolution 24, which calls for the release of the full, unredacted Mueller report and underlying findings to Congress, and House Resolution 430, which authorizes the Committee on the Judiciary to initiate or intervene in judicial proceedings to enforce subpoenas.

Please know that I value the preservation of our democracy and American values above all else. Every day that I serve as your Representative, I am committed to preserving and protecting the Constitution first.

Thank you again for contacting me with your thoughts on this important matter. Your feedback is essential for me to effectively serve as your Representative in Congress. Please continue to share your thoughts, concerns and priorities with me. For additional information on my work in Congress, please sign up for my e-newsletter here.

Sincerely,

Jahana Hayes
Member of Congress"

August 30, 2019

Dear Matthew,

Thank you for contacting me with your thoughts on the impeachment of the President. I appreciate that you took the time to express your thoughts on this matter.

Like you, I deeply respect the Office of the President, and cherish the electoral process that allows an American to assume the Oval Office. I know that the integrity of the presidency, guarded by respect for our foundational laws and values, is more important than any one person or political party. I will always protect the sanctity of our democracy over the consideration of political or electoral implications.

Over the past two years, Special Counsel Mueller's investigation has led to charges filed against 37 individuals, and secured seven guilty pleas and one conviction at trial. Among these were six former associates and advisers of the President; their charges included financial crimes, working with foreign governments, and making false statements to the FBI and Congress.

After reviewing the Special Counsel's report, two things are abundantly clear: the Russian government launched an extended and intentional misinformation campaign to influence the 2016 American presidential election, and the President and members of his campaign apparatus committed egregious acts that undermined our judiciary system, put our national security at risk, and jeopardized the American people's trust in our electoral system.

The report also showed clear evidence that the President made efforts to obstruct the Special Counsel's investigation into this possible collusion. However, citing a longstanding Department of Justice policy that it is unconstitutional to charge a president with a federal crime while they are in office, the Special Counsel did not formally conclude whether or not the President obstructed justice.

As a career history teacher, I know the Constitution, and I know that no one is above the law. The Constitution provides checks and balances to Congress, the Executive branch, and the Judiciary to ensure that no branch of government can violate American laws and foundations without being held accountable. In the most serious cases, the Constitution entrusts Congress with the power to file articles of impeachment and remove a President from office – and these are serious times.

The President's behavior is not becoming of the Oval Office, and he has even said that he would take information from a foreign country if given the opportunity again. I believe that the actions detailed in the Special Counsel's report, along with this behavior, demand the utmost concern and immediate action from Congress. That is why I support a thorough investigation of the President's behavior, whether through the current investigations that my colleagues are leading or through an impeachment inquiry. This will allow Congress to gather all of the necessary information needed.

President Trump's openness to foreign interference is deeply concerning. Congress has a responsibility to investigate what happened in the 2016 election and the administration's actions since that time. Those investigations must continue, and I would support an impeachment inquiry if that is where the facts take us. But first, Congress and the American people need to get all the information required.

Over the past few months, I have voted with my colleagues to pass House Concurrent Resolution 24, which calls for the release of the full, unredacted Mueller report and underlying findings to Congress, and House Resolution 430, which authorizes the Committee on the Judiciary to initiate or intervene in judicial proceedings to enforce subpoenas.

Please know that I value the preservation of our democracy and American values above all else. Every day that I serve as your Representative, I am committed to preserving and protecting the Constitution first.

Thank you again for contacting me with your thoughts on this important matter. Your feedback is essential for me to effectively serve as your Representative in Congress. Please continue to share your thoughts, concerns and priorities with me. For additional information on my work in Congress, please sign up for my e-newsletter here.

Sincerely,

Jahana Hayes

Jahana Hayes
Member of Congress

Here is the generic email:

"Since coming to Congress, my mission has been clear: to open up the doors of access and opportunity for all my constituents, especially those that have felt cut out of the process or the benefits that federal government can provide.

That mission extends beyond introducing legislation or voting for bills on the House floor.

My office can serve as your front door to the federal government, helping you with issues you may encounter with the Social Security Administration, Veterans Administration, and United States Citizenship and Immigration Services, among others.

I have designated talented staff in my Waterbury, CT office to helping you with these issues.

Don't just take it from me- take it from constituents who have already reached out to my office. RC, from Danbury, saved $1,339 in medical bills when my office fixed an issue with his Medicare benefit start date. Danielle, a resident of the Danbury Federal Correctional Institution, was able to secure a dental appointment for a festering cavity because of the actions of my office. Her friend, who referred her to me, said,

'I'm confident that, without the assistance of Representative Hayes, Danielle would not have received her temporary filling and likely eventually would have lost that tooth.' Having a problem with a federal agency?

I can help you HERE.
Are you applying for a federal grant, or want more information on what may be available for you?

I can help you HERE.

Interested in taking tours of the White House, the Capitol, the Supreme Court, and more while in DC?

I can help you <u>HERE</u>."[3]

---

[3]Representative Jahana Hayes. CT05JH.Outreach@mail.house.gov. Email communication. August 13. 2019.

The only means of attracting the attention of your representatives is as follows: (1) to pay (direct campaign contribution or lobbyist); (2) send a massive volume of written correspondence[4] and/or (3) sue in federal or state court.

Otherwise, as my community learned through the legal discovery process for spent reactor fuel storage, you are *materially worthless* (or worth approximately $4,000.00 per person/per fatality) to the United States government.

Knowing in advance that <u>very few individuals and their professional staff members</u> would respond to my letters directly, unless I was paying them (via a campaign contribution) and/or a lobbyist (corporate donation) and/or suing in state or federal court, the letters instead served to formulate my own position on public policy issues.

The message to readers is clear: You must pay or litigate for your message to be heard. Despite this ultimatum: Send your letters anyway.

---

[4]The $300 to $400 expense for postage for a legal letter may be cost prohibitive for a diabled veteran, a senior on fixed income and/or a family in Section 8 housing.

You shouldn't be discouraged by the <u>pay-to-play</u> nature of the United States government. Learn to be an agile fighter. Practice your defense and offense. Every opponent has a weakness. The hunted can become the hunters. David did triumph in the end.

If for some reason you don't win readers: Leave the United States. Become a citizen of another country. Take your assets and wealth elsewhere. The world is a large and complex place. The cycling and pedestrian friendly (café) life of Europe may be more to your liking. The skiing or snowboarding of Switzerland might be more attractive. The football culture of South America may be seductive. The surfing of the Pacific may draw you away. The relaxing high- speed rail commuting of Japan or Europe may lure you away instead of the forty years (and counting) of Los Angeles car traffic gridlock.[5]

---

[5]Note: Los Angeleans should expect to waste trillions of hours of time (and billions of gallons of gasoline) in traffic (sitting at a complete standstill) over the next forty years. In the year 2059 traffic will be the same or worse).

Other countries may value your experiences and skill sets more than the United States does. Again if you find yourself thinking that the infrastructure (including, but not limited to, Flint, Michigan[6] and Newark, New Jersey) of this country is worse than most war torn *unstable* 3rd world countries: Why stay? There is nothing keeping you here.

David also has the option of tossing his slingshot in a backpack, boarding a plane (or boat) and leaving a dysfunctional place. Why bother fighting Goliath when other countries offer relaxing high-speed rail to work, café life and cycling friendly conditions?

The underlying conclusion for those readers that may be dissatisfied with the conditions in the United States: Don't give up hope (or engage in rash behavior) if you haven't beaten Goliath. Make a change. The world is a large place.

---

[6]Flint, Michigan was actually used for urban military warzone training purposes. *Army calls cease-fire on military exercises that rattled Flint.* Ron Fonger. MLive. Jun 11, 2015.
https://www.mlive.com/news/flint/2015/06/military_exercises_over_i n_fli.html.

Addendum - Letters Received Post Publication

In fairness to the professional staff members of Congresswoman Jahana Hayes (Ocean Debris) and Senator Tim Kaine (Impeachment) the following letters are being included in a 2nd edition.

September 11, 2019

Dear Matthew,

Thank you for contacting me about the *Save Our Seas (SOS) 2.0 Act*. I appreciate hearing your thoughts on this important matter.

As you may know, the *Save Our Seas 2.0 Act* was introduced by Senator Sullivan (AL) in the Senate, and by Representative Suzanne Bonamici (OR-1) in the House of Representatives on July 25, 2019. This bill seeks to reduce the creation of plastic waste, find use for plastic waste that already exists to keep it from entering the oceans, and spur innovation into new technologies and ocean-friendly products. This legislation, H.R. 3969, has been referred to the House Committees on Transportation and Infrastructure, Natural Resources, Ways and Means, Foreign Affairs,

Like you, I understand that pollution and its impacts on our environment and wildlife is one of the most pressing issues of our time. Please know that I am working with my colleagues on both sides of the aisle to make progress on this critical issue in the House of Representatives.

Thank you again for contacting me to weigh in on this matter. Your feedback is essential for me to effectively serve as your Representative in Congress. Please continue to share your opinions, concerns and priorities with me. To keep up with my work in Congress, please sign up for my e-newsletter here.

Sincerely,

Jahana Hayes
Member of Congress

Post publication letter on Oceans Debris – Jahana Hayes.

TIM KAINE
VIRGINIA

COMMITTEE ON
ARMED SERVICES

COMMITTEE ON
FOREIGN RELATIONS

COMMITTEE ON
THE BUDGET

COMMITTEE ON
HEALTH, EDUCATION, LABOR,
AND PENSIONS

WASHINGTON OFFICE:

WASHINGTON, DC 20510-4607
(202) 224-4024

United States Senate
WASHINGTON, DC 20510-4607

August 22, 2019

Mr Matthew Myers
PO Box 289
Lakeville, CT 06039-0289

Dear Mr Myers.

Thank you for contacting me. I appreciate hearing from you.

On April 18, 2019, Attorney General William Barr released to the public a redacted version of Special Counsel Robert Mueller's report on the investigation into Russia's involvement in the 2016 presidential election and possible links to the Trump campaign. Prior to the release of the report, the probe led to numerous high-profile indictments and guilty pleas of the President's associates.

The report establishes, yet again, that Russia interfered in the 2016 election to help then-candidate Donald Trump. Trump encouraged the attack, and members of his campaign celebrated it. The report also cites a great deal of evidence in support of an obstruction of justice charge and other cases of serious misconduct by the President.

Special Counsel Mueller's July 24, 2019 testimony before the House Intelligence and Judiciary committees echoed to the American people that he did not exonerate the President of the multiple acts of misconduct committed during and after his election. The House is now sifting through the evidence to ensure Congress fulfills its oversight duties.

I've heard from many who have inquired about the Presidential impeachment process provided by the Constitution. A simple majority in the House of Representatives has the authority to determine and approve articles of impeachment against the President, Vice President, or other federal officers. If the grounds for impeachment are agreed to by the House, they are sent to the Senate, where members have the authority to conduct a trial. A conviction can only be reached if two-thirds of the Senate agrees on any article.

The integrity of our elections is one of the most pressing issues facing our country and democracy Special Counsel Mueller's testimony reaffirmed that Russia interfered in the 2016 presidential election in sweeping and systematic fashion. Mr Mueller stated that along with Russia, other foreign actors are working to destabilize our elections with misinformation campaigns, similar to Russia's interference model. This should be a bipartisan issue; it is something that can directly affect our democracy We need to debate and pass bills that protect election integrity, develop a national strategy for combatting these attacks, and ensure that what happened in 2016 cannot and will not happen again.

The key findings of the Mueller Report have, appropriately, sparked strong reactions from the American public. I commend Mr Mueller for doing his job thoroughly while under constant criticism by the President. I have also heard from many constituents who have expressed disillusionment with Attorney General Barr's handling of the report, including reports that the Department of Justice discussed Mueller's finding with the White House prior to its public release.

Post publication letter on Impeachment - Senator Tim Kaine – Page 1.

Please be assured that I will continue to push for increased transparency around this investigation and that I will always fight to preserve our nation's sovereignty and the system of checks and balances that entrusts true power to the people. Thank you again for contacting me.

Sincerely,

Tim Kaine

Post publication letter on Impeachment - Senator Tim Kaine – Page 2.

www.ingramcontent.com/pod-product-compliance
Lightning Source LLC
Chambersburg PA
CBHW041716200326
41519CB00005B/274